How to Care for Your Kitten

CONTENTS

Photos by:
Frank Naylor,
Colin Jeal,
Alan Robinson,
Jeff Spall,
Nick Mays

©2001 by Kingdom Books PO9 5TT ENGLAND
Printed in China through Printworks Int. Ltd.

INTRODUCTION

Kittens! Who can resist their charm? Small and cuddly, full of mischief, and easy to care for. Yet a kitten is a living creature which will soon grow into a cat. For this reason, you should never acquire a kitten without very careful consideration. This book will tell you the basics of kitten care.

Today the cat is Great Britain's 'top pet', having overtaken the dog in the popularity stakes. It is true that a cat often fits better into today's busy lifestyle. Even if you spend several hours a day away from home at work or school you can keep a cat as a pet (or, even better, two cats). The cat will be content to be on its own for a large part of the day.

The cat is easy to care for, and has many endearing qualities which make it a delightful pet.

The cat is an excellent companion for young and old alike. Children who are allowed to grow up with kittens in the home will learn to

American-style Chinchilla Persians, like this 12-week-old kitten, are slightly darker and have more luxuriant coats than their British counterparts.

respect life and to be caring - provided that they are properly supervised, of course. My eldest daughter did not find it difficult to adjust to sharing her home, parents and toys when her little sister was born, simply because she was already used to sharing with her beloved cats!

There is a cat or kitten to suit everyone. There are many different breeds and colours, as well as the common, lovable pet cat that can take almost any shape and colour. A cat can be kept purely as an indoor pet (if used to this from kittenhood), perhaps doubling as a show animal, or as a hunter to rid your home of unwanted pests such as mice and rats. No matter why you decide to keep a cat it will inevitably become a vital part of the family. Chosen with care and consideration, your new kitten will easily adapt to your particular lifestyle. On top of all this, a cat is relatively inexpensive both to buy and to keep, and it has a lifespan of 15 years or more. Is it any wonder that cats are our most popular pets?

SELECTION

Many cat owners will tell you that they never actually selected their cat: it selected them! You may find a stray cat in your garden and decide to give it a home, or in your neighbour's unplanned litter, or you may come by your kitten in any number of other ways. With a little care, this can work out very well indeed, but please never take on a kitten just because it is so cute and appealing. Do make sure that you will be able to care properly for a cat for all of its natural life. Are there other members of your family that may not welcome a kitten? Is somebody close to you allergic to cats? Are you house-

It is easy to fall for a small, appealing kitten, but are you prepared to care for it for the whole of its natural life?

A delightful six-week-old kitten. Non-pedigree kittens should not be sold until they are at least eight (preferably ten) weeks old. Pedigrees should be twelve weeks.

proud to the extent that you would consider scratch marks on your new furniture to be a disaster? Think carefully before you bring a kitten home, to avoid the heartbreak, for you and the kitten, if you have to part with it later on.

There are thousands of unwanted cats in Britain, many of which are having to be put to sleep by animal charities simply because there are not enough good homes available. Many of these cats have been discarded for one of the above reasons, or simply because the novelty of owning a kitten wore off when it was no longer quite so small and cute. By taking on a kitten, you should be committing yourself to caring for that cat for life.

Pedigree or Non-Pedigree?

Most people will simply opt for a non-pedigree, sometimes affectionately called a 'moggy', and these make marvellous pets for millions of people. Non-pedigree kittens are easy to come by, and will be very inexpensive to buy, often being offered as 'free to good homes'.The very best place, however, from which to obtain your non-pedigree kitten is your local animal shelter, or Cats Protection League. The staff will be able to help you select a suitable kitten, and they can also give you advice regarding its care. Be prepared to answer several questions yourself, as the shelter will need to make sure that you are suitable as a cat owner. The kittens at a shelter will have been checked over by a vet, so you can be reasonably certain that you will acquire a healthy kitten - something which is not always the case when you pick a kitten from the litter down the road. You will also do the kitten a big favour by giving it a loving home.

Do please also bear in mind that there are many adult cats in shelters all over the country, waiting for new homes. An adult cat can make just as good a pet as a kitten.

If you would prefer to buy a pedigree kitten, then you will need to do some research beforehand. A pedigree kitten has one advantage over the non-pedigree: you will be able to predict what its behaviour and temperament will be like as an adult, as most

A seven-week-old Blue Cream Persian kitten.

Shaded Silver Persian. The Shaded Silver is a darker version of the Chinchilla.

individuals within one particular breed follow the same basic behaviour pattern. If you want a well-bred cat of a particular appearance that will have a temperament to suit you and your family, then opt for a pedigree kitten. A pedigree kitten will cost considerably more (often several hundred pounds) but you must bear in mind that you are paying for the knowledge that you have a carefully bred and reared kitten, from parents that have been tested for serious diseases, which will grow up just as you want it: a loving, quiet lap cat or vocal, playful extrovert. A pedigree kitten will also have had its inoculations by the time you buy it, which is seldom if ever the case with non-pedigrees.

Pedigree Breeds

There are several breed groups of pedigree cat:

The Longhairs: all the Persian cats. These come in nearly a hundred different colours and colour combinations. There are self-coloured Persians whose coats consist of one colour only, such as Black, Blue, Cream or White.There are Bi-colours that are marked with white, such as Black and white or Red and white. There are Tabbies and Smokes, Tortoiseshell and silver coloured Chinchillas. One of the most popular Persian varieties is the Colourpoint, where the cat is marked like a Siamese. Persian cats have cobby bodies, with small ears and flat faces. Their long, flowing coats need daily care. They are gentle, quiet and affectionate.

The Exotic: a shorthaired version of the Persian.

The Semi-Longhair: cats whose long coats are not as long as those of the Persians, and so they do not need the same amount of grooming. Slightly more lively than the Persian, but still affectionate, and with a much longer face, semi-longhairs include Birmans (with Siamese markings and white 'socks'), Turkish Vans (white cats with coloured tails and patches around their ears), Maine Coons (a very large, wild-looking breed) and Ragdolls (known for their even temperament and innocent of the charge of genetic disorder which is often levelled against them).

The British Shorthair: the pedigree version of the usual sturdy, non-pedigree cat with no exaggerated attributes. British Shorthairs are very popular as pets and come in many colour varieties, the most popular of which is the British Blue. Other colours include Black, Cream, White, Tabby, Bi-colour and the very pretty British Tipped: a silver-coloured cat like the Chinchilla Persian.

The Siamese Cat: long and sleek, with large ears and a long, thin tail. The face is wedge-shaped, with deep blue eyes. The body colour is pale, with darker face mask, legs, tail and ears. Far from just existing in one colour, as is sometimes believed (the most common colour being the Seal Point, where the 'points' are nearly black) there are 26 different point colours to choose from, including Blue Point, Lilac Point, Red Point and various Tabby Points. The Siamese is a lively extrovert with a very loud voice. It is a highly intelligent cat which will easily become bored, so it needs plenty of stimulation, preferably in the form of another Siamese companion. There is also a semi-longhaired version of the Siamese: the Balinese.

The Burmese: somewhere between the Siamese and the British Shorthair: not quite as slender as the Siamese, yet without the size and mass of the British. Burmese are similar to Siamese in temperament, and they come in colours such as Blue, Red, Cream, Tortoiseshell and Brown.

Foreign Breeds: include the pretty and affectionate Abyssinian, a shorthaired breed with a slightly wedge-shaped face that comes in its natural 'wild' colour (known as Usual), a pretty red known as Sorrel, Blue and a couple more. There is also a semi-longhaired version known as the Somali. Two very distinctive foreign breeds (although originating in Britain) are the Cornish Rex and the Devon Rex. These cats have slender bodies covered in curly, soft fur. They

Are you going to allow your cat to go outside? This kitten is obviously happy in the garden, but many cats are content to stay indoors all the time.

are affectionate and lively. Other Foreigns are the two blue-coloured shorthaired breeds: the Russian Blue and the Korat.

Finally, the **Oriental group** consists of cats which are shaped just like Siamese, with the same temperament and behaviour, but which are the same colour or shading all over. They can be white, such as in the Foreign White, black, as in the Oriental Black, spotted tabby, as in the Oriental Spotted, or many other colours.

Whether you have decided on a pedigree or non-pedigree, take care that your choice is a friendly, healthy kitten. First of all, no kitten should have to leave its mother too soon unless it is an orphan. Sadly, many non-pedigree kittens are sold when they are much too young. A kitten taken too soon from its mother will feel very insecure and retain something of this throughout its life. A non-pedigree kitten should be about eight weeks old when you buy it. Pedigree kittens, slightly slower to mature than non-pedigrees, are usually sold at 10 to 12 weeks. The kitten that you pick should be friendly and inquisitive. Avoid the nervous kitten that is hiding; it may grow up to be an equally nervous adult. It should have clear, bright eyes, clean fur and ears, a nose with no signs of discharge, and its body should feel firm, neither thin nor fat. A dirty kitten should be rejected. Cats are, by nature, extremely clean animals and they wash themselves continually, so a dirty kitten that cannot be bothered to wash is very likely to be unhealthy.

Male or Female

Which sex you choose is of little importance, as males and females both make equally loving pets. Any kitten not intended for breeding (which should include all non-pedigrees) should be neutered at a suitable age, usually around six months. An unneutered cat is a nuisance that will soil your house and may give rise to unplanned, unwanted kittens unless carefully supervised.

Adult Chinchilla Persian of the British type. If you groom your Longhair kitten it will accept the process as an adult, when its coat becomes really thick.

One or Two?

The simple answer to this question is: two! Two kittens will not mean much more work than one, and each will be much happier with feline company. Two kittens allowed to grow up together will be friends for life

Bringing Your Kitten(s) Home

Always use a good quality cat carrier for transportation, even if you live just down the road.

Put a soft blanket or towel inside the carrier to make your kitten as comfortable as possible. Make sure that this is washable, just in case the kitten has a little accident. If you are travelling by car, make sure that the kitten has not been fed recently in case of travel sickness. When travelling, put the cat carrier on your lap, and talk softly to the kitten, gently reassuring it that everything is all right. Your kitten will naturally feel rather worried, having left its mother and litter-mates behind.

Having arrived home, select a quiet spot and put the cat carrier on the floor. Open the door of the carrier, and leave it like that. The kitten will then be able to venture out in its own time. Make sure that water, food and litter tray are all close at hand. Do not be tempted to handle your kitten too much during the first day, as it will need some time to get used to its new environment. There will soon be plenty of time for cuddles. Most kittens will settle in happily within a couple of days. If you have other pets, such as a dog or another cat, you must supervise introductions carefully, never leaving the kitten on its own with the other pet until you are sure that they are going to be friends. Similarly, when there are young children in the house, make sure that they know how to handle the kitten correctly, and that they do not handle it constantly. Like all babies, young kittens need plenty of sleep.

The following is a list of equipment that you will need for your kitten.

Cat Carrier: The best type is made of plastic, with a door of metal or traditional wicker. This type is secure and easy to clean, and comes in many different sizes. A cat carrier is an absolute 'must' for transporting your cat, from its breeder to its new home for example, or for trips to the vet.

Litter Tray: Even a cat that is allowed outdoors will benefit from a litter tray, for example for use when the weather is bad.

Food and Water Bowls: These should be easy to clean and

Some of the equipment you will need for your kitten.

preferably unbreakable. The best type is the light-weight metal bowl, available in many different sizes.

Combs and Brushes: Exactly what you need will depend on whether your kitten is shorthaired, longhaired or semi-longhaired. (See the section on Grooming.)

Scratching Post: A 'must' for the cat that is to spend all its time indoors. If your new kitten is presented with a scratching post as soon as it arrives it will get used to the concept of exercising its claws on this rather than on your best furniture. If you delay the purchase of a scratching post the kitten may scratch your furniture, and will then be reluctant to use a scratching post instead. Scratching posts come in many shapes and sizes, from a small plain board covered in carpet or rope to elaborate 'cat trees' with several platforms onto which the cat can climb. Buy the one you can afford.

Toys: Kittens love toys. There are many available in pet shops, and the ones impregnated with catnip tend to be particularly popular. There is no real need to spend money on toys, however, as a kitten will play happily with an empty cotton reel, a ping-pong ball, a pine cone or a screwed up piece of paper. Just use your imagination.

Collar and Disc: If your kitten is to be allowed outdoors it must wear a collar and disc in case it gets lost. The collar should be partly elasticated to prevent strangulation if the kitten gets caught up somewhere. The disc should show your telephone number and address so that people can contact you if your kitten gets lost.

Bed: This is not really a necessary item as most cats and kittens are happy to sleep anywhere. If you do want to buy a bed for your kitten, there are many designs to choose from, but do not expect your kitten to sleep in it all the time. You cannot force a cat to sleep in one particular place!

'Champagne Charlie', another award-winning rescued cat belonging to Linda Jones.

FEEDING

Cats are obligate carnivores, which means that they cannot survive without meat.

Young kittens have very small stomachs, but need a lot of protein and other nutrients to be able to grow and develop. Because of this, a kitten has to be fed a concentrated diet, which will usually mean a specially formulated kitten food.

If you are at all unsure, ask your veterinary surgeon for advice on feeding. You should not attempt to feed either kittens or cats on home-cooked food as it is unlikely that the animals will receive all the necessary nutrients from such a diet. When provided with food specially formulated for kittens or cats your cat will need no extra vitamin supplements. Always choose a good quality food with a well-known brand name, as cheap cat food often contains a considerable amount of cereal and not enough protein to keep your cat healthy.

A kitten up to the age of six months will need four meals a day. From six to nine months three meals should be served. Two meals a day will suffice once the cat has reached nine months and therefore officially become an adult.

It is best to give weaned kittens and adult cats water to drink, as they will have no need for milk. If you prefer to give milk make sure to use milk manufactured especially for cats, as cow's milk will often give cats and kittens upset stomachs.

A kitten up to the age of six months will need four meals a day.

Cats are very independent animals, and are therefore very difficult to train.

What all cats will need to know is how to be clean in the house. This will mean either using a litter tray, or going outside. Usually there is no need whatsoever to teach a kitten to use a litter tray. Nearly all kittens will have been taught by their mother, even if the mother. Just show the kitten where the tray is and the rest should follow. Make sure that it is placed in a quiet corner of the house, and that it is kept clean. Cats are normally very clean animals and, if they find their litter tray in a dirty state, they may decide to do their business somewhere else in the house.

If you want your cat to perform out of doors, the easiest way to achieve this is to place the litter tray by the door, and eventually to move it into the garden, disposing of it once the cat has got the idea. However, as mentioned earlier, even an outdoor cat will need an indoor litter tray at times.

The only other training that you will need or be able to do is to teach your kitten its name, and how to behave in the house. Use your kitten's name during play sessions and when calling it to dinner and it will soon learn to respond. As regards behaviour in the house, you may want the kitten to keep off certain raised areas such as the kitchen surfaces and table, and you may not want it to get on your bed. This can be difficult to achieve, not to say impossible. If your kitten ever jumps up where you don't want it, clap your hands and

say 'No'. With luck, and perseverance on your part, the kitten will learn. However, if you do not manage to teach it your best option will be to keep the door to that room closed.

A seven-week-old Blue Cream Persian kitten.

GROOMING

How much grooming your kitten will need is dependent upon its type of coat. Naturally, a longhaired Persian will require much more grooming than a sleek-coated Siamese, or a non-pedigree shorthair. But whatever type of cat you have, it is important to get your kitten used to being groomed from as early an age as possible. Your longhaired kitten may not have a tremendous amount of fur, but one day it will, and it is no use kidding yourself that an adult cat will accept combing and brushing if it did not learn to accept it as a kitten. Grooming your kitten should be part of its routine care and serves to enhance the friendship between the kitten and you, its owner.

Shorthaired cats will just need the occasional brushing with a soft-bristle brush, or one made of rubber. By brushing your cat you will remove old, dead hairs that need to come out, which is especially important when the cat is moulting. A cat is a very clean animal that spends a lot of time washing itself. In doing so it will inevitably swallow some fur. If too much fur is swallowed a fur ball will form in the intestines. Usually, the cat will dispose of this by vomiting, but occasionally a fur ball may become stuck and need veterinary treatment. By grooming your cat you will help to prevent it from swallowing too much fur.

Semi-longhaired cats, including most longhaired non-pedigrees, will need combing and brushing once or twice a week. Use a fine-toothed metal comb and a soft-bristle brush to finish off. Pay special attention to the areas behind the cat's ears, on its hind-legs and between its legs, as this is where knots and tangles will form. An occasional sprinkle of non-perfumed baby powder (or special grooming powder for cats) will help keep the coat soft and free of grease.

Persian cats need a lot of careful grooming. How much depends on the individual cat. Some have heavy, dense coats that need to be groomed every day to keep them tangle free; others have less heavy coats and will be all right with twice-weekly groomings. For a Persian, you will need at least two combs (one wide-toothed and one fine-toothed metal) and a soft-bristle brush.

Start the grooming process with the wide-toothed comb. Once that moves freely through the fur, switch to the fine-toothed comb to untangle any knots that the wide-toothed comb may have missed. Finish off by using the brush. Areas requiring particular attention include the so-called ruff on the chest, the area around the cat's ears, the hind-legs and the whole tummy area. Persian cats will benefit greatly from being 'powder groomed' every now and then. Rub a small amount of non-perfumed powder into the coat and then brush it out again. Persians also need to be bathed regularly. A Persian whose fur gets matted very easily is probably suffering from excess oils in the coat, and these will be removed by bathing. An ungroomed Persian is a very sorry sight and may even have to be taken to the vet's to be shaved under general anaesthetic: never be tempted to leave out the grooming session even for a week or so.

Eyes And Ears

Normally, a healthy cat's eyes need little or no attention. If some crusty discharge has formed underneath the eye, gently wipe this off with a damp piece of cotton wool or a special eye-wipe available

from pet shops and vets. Flat-faced cats such as Persians often have runny eyes as a matter of course, and this is nothing to worry about unduly. As long as the eye itself is clear and is not sore, just wipe away the residue every day. If your cat's eyes ever appear sore or inflamed, see a vet. Most cats will not need to have their ears cleaned if they are healthy. Never attempt

A cat is a very clean animal that spends a lot of time washing itself.

to clean an ear that looks healthy, as the disturbance may actually cause problems. Some cats, especially those with a lot of fur inside their ears, will suffer from a lot of earwax. This is grey in colour and very greasy. Wipe it off from the outer ear with some cotton wool or a special ear-wipe, but do not touch the ear further down.

Only if the ear appears sore (for instance, if the cat is scratching it a lot, or holding it folded down) should you clean the ear canal itself, and then only after you have sought veterinary advice.

A blue Tonkinese kitten.

Teeth

Nearly all cats will start to get a build-up of tartar on their teeth from about the age of one year. Outdoor cats which regularly catch and eat rats and mice tend to be fairly tartar free because of the strenuous exercise their teeth get. This, however, is no reason for actively encouraging your cat to catch prey, which can lead to other problems, such as worms and fleas. If you see a build-up of brown matter on your cat's teeth, let your vet descale them. If it is left untreated, tartar will eventually cause gum disease and tooth loss.

A 12-week-old Red Tabby Persian kitten.

Claws

A cat that is allowed out should not have its claws clipped. It will need them sharp to climb and to defend itself. An indoor cat may benefit from regular trimming of its claws, and so will your furniture! Using nail scissors or claw-trimmers sold especially for cats, snip the sharp tip off each claw. You need not cut more than the actual tip as cats' claws seldom overgrow, and the process will have to be repeated regularly as the sharp tip will regrow within a week or so.

Bathing

The rule of thumb is: if your cat is so dirty that it cannot clean itself properly it needs a bath. Persian cats will certainly need regular baths, about one a month. Use a shampoo intended for cats; never use dog shampoo, or human shampoo (with the possible exception of baby shampoo). Put the cat in the bath, in the sink or in a large bowl, preferably with a rubber mat at the bottom to stop it from slipping. Wet the coat thoroughly with lukewarm water, using either a hand-held shower attachment or a jug. Avoid getting water into the eyes and ears. Next, gently massage the shampoo into the coat, taking extra care around the tail area which may need extra cleaning. Then rinse the cat until its coat is completely free of shampoo. Squeeze any excess water out of the coat, then towel it dry. If your cat will let you use a hair-dryer, do so; otherwise, keep the cat in a warm room near a radiator or fire until it is dry. Cats that have been used to baths since kittenhood seldom object too much.

You will want to keep your kitten as healthy as possible. To maintain your cat's health, make sure that it:

- receives a good diet.
- is getting annual booster vaccinations and check-ups at the vet's.
- is kept clean and well groomed.

All cats need to be vaccinated against cat influenza and feline enteritis, and this has to be repeated annually. Your cat could fall ill and die if you do not have it vaccinated, even if it is kept indoors permanently. Viruses can be transferred to your cat through your shoes, for example, if you have been walking in an affected area. These days it is also possible to vaccinate against Feline Leukaemia Virus (FeLV) and Feline Chlamydia, although this is of less benefit if your cat is an indoor cat. Discuss the options with your vet.

Some common feline disorders include:

Fleas: Sometimes you will actually see the fleas themselves sprint through your cat's fur, but more often the presence of flea-dirt (small black specks that go red when moistened) will be evidence enough to prove that your cat has fleas. Many different types of flea treatment are available, such as sprays, flea collars, and special flea drops to put on the cat's neck.

A brown tabby and white male Maine Coon kitten.

There are even pills you can give the cat to prevent fleas. Discuss the options with your vet; some flea treatments will be available only from vets.

Worms: Cats get worms by eating rats, mice and birds and by swallowing fleas when grooming themselves, and kittens can become infected by their mother while still in the womb. The two most common types of worm are the roundworm and the tapeworm. Symptoms of worms may include a dull coat and distended belly with a thin body, and worms can sometimes actually be seen in the cat's fur, around the tail or in its faeces. Your vet will sell the best worming treatments available. Different types of worm need different treatment, so always consult your vet.

Ear Mites: Seen as a black, crusty discharge inside your cat's ears. Causes considerable itching, and will spread to other pets such as dogs. See your vet for treatment, which will usually involve eardrops.

Diarrhoea: Can be caused by a change in diet, or as a symptom of any of a number of diseases. If your cat suffers from diarrhoea, leave it without food, but with access to water, for 24 hours to give the stomach a rest. Once the stomach has settled, give the cat a gentle diet of boiled fish, turkey or chicken. If all is well, you can then gradually start to introduce the cat's normal diet into the food, but not too much at a time. If the diarrhoea persists, see a vet.

Always see a vet if you are at all uncertain about your cat's health.

As you can see, the Exotic Shorthair is like a Persian, but with short hair. If you buy
a pedigree kitten you will have some idea what it will look like when it grows up.

BREEDING

The breeding of cats is not something which should be undertaken lightly, and it is much too complex a subject to be covered in a book of this size. As a general rule, cat breeding should be left to the experts. Non-pedigrees should not be bred from, simply because there are already so many cats in desperate need of good homes. Please do not add to the problem; have your cat neutered. It is only an old wives' tale that a female cat (queen) should be bred from before being neutered. She will receive no benefit from this at all. Rather the opposite: if bred from and then neutered she may pine for kittens for the rest of her life.

Pedigree kittens should only be bred from good quality parents, free from hereditary and infectious diseases (blood tests for checking the possible presence of Feline Leukaemia Virus and Feline Immunodeficiency Virus will be needed before mating) and preferably from parents that are good quality show cats. Breeding from pet quality cats will not produce kittens that are any less nice as pets, but you will find them much more difficult to sell. At the end of the day, it is your responsibility to find good homes for all the kittens, as you were responsible for allowing them to be brought into the world.

Cat breeding also involves considerable expense, such as veterinary fees, stud fees if you do not have your own male cat (and if you do he will need his own purpose-built stud quarters outside), feeding the queen and kittens, and fees for vaccinating and registering the kittens. The price of a pedigree kitten may seem like a good incentive to breed, but believe me, you seldom, if ever, make a profit. The expenses nearly always outweigh the income.

A pedigree Maine Coon tabby kitten.

BIBLIOGRAPHY

KITTENS
by Greg Ovechka
ISBN 0-7938-3043-5
RD-003
It's hard to find anyone who does not love kittens - those irresistible, pouncing bundles of fluff. However, enjoying a kitten and seeing it thrive involves more than just buying a toy mouse and a food bowl. This book guides the owner through such topics as selecting a kitten, health care, feeding, choosing a vet and bringing your kitten home.
Hardcover: 180mm x 260mm, 64 pages, full colour photographs throughout.

MOGGIES
by Marianne Mays
ISBN 1-8527-9024-5
GB-011
A book for all owners of non-pedigree cats. Covers all aspects of cat care and also showing non-pedigree cats.
Hardcover: 180mm x 260mm, 128 pages, full colour photographs throughout.

KITTEN AND CAT CARE
by Patricia Paula
ISBN: 0-7938-3046-X
RD-078
Millions of cat-owning households in the world attest to the fact that cats are wonderful pets. Some people love cats because of their independent yet affectionate nature, their grace, or their physical beauty. But cats have so many more great qualities - they do not need to be walked, and they can easily amuse themselves when their human family is not at home. To be a happy and healthy companion, a cat needs a committed and loving owner who is armed with the kind of invaluable cat care advice presented in this book.
Hardcover: 180mm x 260mm, 64 pages, 92 laminated colour photographs.

CAT BEHAVIOUR AND TRAINING
by Dr Lowell Ackerman
ISBN: 0-7938-0634-8
TS-253
Dr Ackerman has brought together the experiences of 20 specialists - vets, behavioural specialists and consultants - to offer their experience about the sort of difficulties cat owners can encounter and how best to overcome them. They provide all that is needed to select the most suitable cat, to train it to be a contributing member of the family and to understand the reasons behind, and deal with, any difficulties that may arise.
Hard cover: 180mm x 260mm, 317 pages, over 200 full colour individually laminated photographs.

For further information see website: www.moggies.co.uk